T0193334

A Pure
And
Clear Thought

Balboa Press books may be ordered through booksellers or by contacting:

Balboa Press
A Division of Hay House
1663 Liberty Drive
Bloomington, IN 47403
www.balboapress.com
844-682-1282

Designs and Images created by the author

ISBN: 978-1-9822-6498-7 (sc)
ISBN: 978-1-9822-6499-4 (e)

Print information available on the last page.

Balboa Press rev. date: 03/18/2021

BALBOA.PRESS
A DIVISION OF HAY HOUSE

Contents

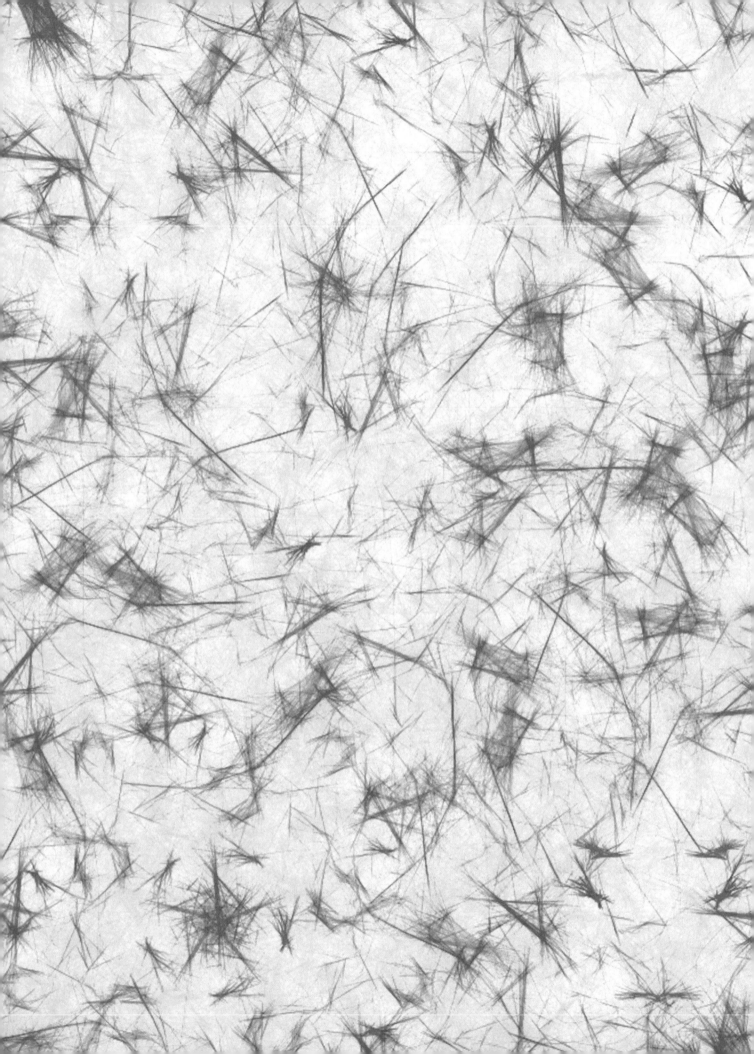

HOW TO LIVE

If we had known the date of our death
Then we'll spend all of our wealth

If we all know that we always have to share
Then there will not be poverty anywhere

If no junk food will be available anywhere
Then half of the sickness will be gone from everywhere

If we know how to love, faith and respect
Then there will not be cruelty to the greater extent

If Christmas gifts will be given to the people we hate
Then our hearts will be changed, we just have to wait

If birthday gifts will be given to poor, lame and sick
Then how to live this life, we will learn that quick

WORRY

Worry about your body
Because you get that only once

Worry about your Lord
Because he may get some complaints

Worry about your neighbors
Because they are the ones most near and dear to you

Worry about your family members
Because you always have to be with them

Worry about your religion
Because it will show you the path to Lord

Worry about your time
Because it is not going to come back

A CHALLENGE FROM THE SUN

I have been living forever
No one can live like me

You can touch my rays
But can never catch me

I have given you life
What have you given me?

You can not live without me
And can never destroy me

I do not become old
You can not stay young like me

I am the brightest bulb in the world
No light bulb can compare to me

I give light to the whole universe
Have you done something like me?

CHANGE

If all of my friends can help one of my friends
Then I know we stand united

If all of my relatives can help one of my relatives
Then I understand we are made equal

If all of my neighbors can help one of my neighbors
Then I think we make a difference

If all of my students can help one of my students
Then I say that we learn a lot from our education

Many drops of rain can make a sea
Many leaves can make a tree

If all of my people can take responsibility of this world
Then I agree that we bring heaven on this earth

I THOUGHT...

I thought I could stop the time with my own hands
But I forgot
Time does not stop for anyone

I thought I could move the globe in my way
But I forgot
Globe has its own speed

I thought I could make the moon much brighter
But I forgot
Moon follows the rules of nature

I thought I could give longer life to the flowers
But I forgot
They will never listen to me

I thought I could give shorter life to the thorns
But I forgot
Sadness endlessly exists in this world

WHENEVER...

Whenever I look at the flower
I see there is no life after this hour

Whenever I look at the thorns
I feel that sorrows may have very strong horns

Whenever I look at the earth
I realize that peace can always be given to birth

Whenever I look at the sea
I like to sit in a boat and have a cup of tea

Whenever I look at the dove
I understand why music cannot be made without love

IF I WERE A PRESIDENT...

If I were a God
Sickness in this world would be cured

If I were a millionnaire
No poor would there be anywhere

If I were a president
A house would be owned by everyone and they'd pay no rent

If I were a celebrity
The role would be played by each personality

If I were a bird
Traveling would be possible anywhere in this world

If I were an actress
This life definitely would not be a mess

O GOD

You have given me everything
But yet have not given me anything

You have given me this beautiful world
But yet have not given me wings to fly

You have given me the good life
But yet have not given me the date of my death

You have given me two hands
But yet have not given me a miraculous power

You have given me many plants
But yet have not given me a dollar tree

You have given me all four seasons
But yet have not given me a remote to change weather

Thanks for what you have done for me
But sorry for not doing much for me

I DON'T UNDERSTAND

If one religion is right
Then where other religions will go

If there is no electric power
Then how our body moves

If all men are equal
Then why everyone looks so different

If everyone has to die
Then why we always make our life

If we have heart, mind and soul
Then why we cannot reach our goal

If we all know God is everywhere
Then why we do not see him anywhere

If sun and moon can live forever
Then why we cannot always live ever

A SPECIAL PLACE

I met someone intelligent
Pure hearted and diligent

I met someone hard working
Sitting late hours and doing something

I met someone weird
Out spoken but always cared

I met someone gentle
Very helpful and always sentimental

I was at a funny world
Where most of them were a nerd

I KNOW

I know your love is gentle
But your house should be of no rental

I know your love is special
But marriage should not be a hassle

I know your love is great
But why you always come so late

I know your love is pure
But I still want to be sure

I know your love is doubtless
But why there is always a mess

I know your love is sweet
But what if we not always meet

I know your love is best
But why you make no life and always take rest

FOR YOU...

My garage has a place for you
But my heart has no space for you

My car has a seat for you
But my heart does not beat for you

An instrument has been bought for you
But my song has not been made for you

The frame has been brought for you
But my picture has not been shot for you

My house has a room for you
But I will never broom for you

OH NO!

Whenever I look at your picture
You look like to me a pitcher

Whenever I look at your waist
To be with you is just a waste

Whenever I look at your lips
I definitely can compare with your hips

Whenever I look at your ears
I can not forget them for years

Whenever I look at your eyes
They scare me and make me cry

Tell me how I can praise for you
When I know I have no craze for you

WITHOUT YOU

Without you
I feel I am a tree
Stuck at one place and not go free

Without you
I have not much to do
I just relax and think of you

Without you
My life has become rough
Everything is going to be tough

Without you
Music can not be made
My songs can not be played

Without you
My life is a hell
I can't get out of this well

CHANGE THIS WORLD, TAKE ALL OF THEIR SINS AWAY

Change this world, take all of their sins away
Change bad thoughts of the bad people
Bow the seeds of kindness, wisdom and forgiveness

Change this world, take all of their sins away
Award the prize to the biggest forgiving person
Take the punishment of bad person upon yourself

Change this world, take all of their sins away
Forgive someone's punishment of lifetime imprisonment
Save his heart, mind and soul from dying

Change this world, take all of their sins away
God, sun and moon do not take someone's freedom away
You also break the dream of giving lifetime imprisonment

O LORD

You are nowhere in the universe
But you have been felt everywhere

You have not been seen by anyone
But you have been found in every spirit

You have only one name
But you have been called by different names

You have only one religion
But you have been brought in many religions

It is not possible to be with you
But every effort has been made to receive you

A CHALLENGE BY THE GOD

What animals talk with each other?
No one can understand except me

How many stars are there in the sky?
It can be counted only by me

What colors should be given to the rainbow?
No one knows better than me

I have made this heavenly sky
Can you make something like me?

You can make computers, telephones, cars and airplanes
But you have been made by me

I have given you heat, water, air, earth and eternal fluid
Can you find some time and think of me?

I know all of your deeds from birth to death
Bring up your sins, I will make you free

THANK YOU

Thank you for giving us sun, moon and stars
Where there is a peace and no wars

Thank you for giving us a heavenly sky
Where there is a rainbow and birds can fly

Thank you for giving us a brilliant brain
That can make a car, computer and airplane

Thank you for giving us this beautiful world
Where there are endless trees, animals and people

Thank you for giving us full freedom
You don't stop us, we can do anything we want to

THE WORLD OF MY DREAMS

In the plants kids will be born
There will be dollars and coins on the thorns

We will understand the language of birds
It will make us happy to know their words

Everyone will live upto the same age
They will leave when they are sixty of their age

Everyone will be able to fly
There will not be a need of visa or passport to fly in the sky

There will be a body parts store
No handicapped will be there anymore

I REALLY DON'T UNDERSTAND

If our heart is broken
Then why we don't die

If we know there is a God
Then why we cannot give him a call

If we can talk to someone across the sea
Then why we cannot speak to God beyond the sky

If there is one God in the world
Then why there are so many

If everything is possible for good Lord
Then why a handicapped cannot become a normal human being

LOVE

Love was never very kind
Someone could become blind

Love was never very beautiful
It became cruel and unfaithful

Love was never very pure
Never stayed the same for sure

Love was never very smart
Someone could lose his heart

Love was never very gentle
People in that became mental

WHENEVER I....

Whenever I look at the sun
I wonder it has been held by none

Whenever I look at the star
I like to hold and put it into the jar

Whenever I look at the moon
It tells me to go far and not come soon

Whenever I look at the tree
It tells me to sit under and not go free

Whenever I look at the bird
I can never understand a word

Whenever I look at the sunset
It reminds me of him and make upset

Whenever I feel the air
It makes me fresh and sit on the chair

DEAR GOD

You don't live in doubts
You live in our beliefs

You don't live in the brain
You live in our soul

You don't take anything from us
You are a great giver of five elements

You don't stop us for doing anything
You have given us heart, mind and soul

There is no limit of your blessings
Trees, birds, cities and stars are there countless

THIS IS CHRISTMAS

Let us celebrate Christmas
Walk on the foot prints of Jesus

Let us love our neighbors
Show our affection, appreciation and help them to our best

Let us love who hate us
Break the bridge of bitterness and pray for them

Let us believe in that nothing is impossible
Determine something good and start on doing it now

This is Christmas
Let us give the gift of forgiveness to the people who were not nice to us.

MY DREAMS

Salt and sugar will not be made anywhere
Diabetics and blood pressure will be gone from every where

On Easter Day you will see
When many prisoners will let go free

It will not be possible to make cigarettes anywhere
The problem of cancer will be gone to some extent forever

Christmas Day will be celebrated as a Forgiveness Day
We will ask for forgiveness and we will be forgiven that day

Real education will be given in the schools
The classes of health and religion will be held every year in the schools